SUCCESS IS NO ACCIDENT

SUCCESS IS NO ACCIDENT

SUCCESS IS NO ACCIDENT

Dr. Lair Ribeiro

St. Martin's Press
New York

 For information, address St. Martin's Press, 175 Fifth Avenue, New York, N.Y. 10010.

Design by Michael Mendelsohn of MM Design 2000, Inc.

Library of Congress Cataloging-in-Publication Data

Ribeiro, Lair.
Success is no accident / by Lair Ribeiro.—1st ed.
p. cm.
Translated from the Portuguese.
ISBN 0-312-14425-3
1. Success—Psychological aspects. I. Title.
BF637.S8R4455 1996
158'.1—dc20 96-6987
CIP

First published in Brazil under the title *O sucesso não ocorre por acaso* by Editora Objetiva, 1992.

First Edition: August 1996

10 9 8 7 6 5 4 3 2 1

CONTENTS

ILLUSTRATIONS

INTRODUCTION

What you are about to read can change your life. This book distills and refines complex ideas about the fundamentals of success into simple and usable messages. The wisdom offered within these pages has been honed from the latest scientific thinking on how we can reach our highest potential, including the basic principles of learning theory, lateral thinking, Gestalt, accelerated learning, and neuro-linguistic programming. I have rendered these complicated theories in their essence: They are offered here to help you use your conscious and unconscious mind's potential to better understand how to take action toward your dreams and goals.

The visual images, metaphors, and stories offered here are tools by which you will learn the principles of success. These words and images are not merely illustrations of my points; rather, they are communications that bypass your critical consciousness to get to the part of your unconscious brain where you are inspired to make real change. Moreover, these visual images appear on the left-hand page wherever possible so as to go directly to the right brain and access your unconscious.

Each chapter is accompanied by a principle of success. These principles are not summaries of chapters but are complete, self-contained units in themselves. They offer another, more poetic way of retaining the deeper meaning of the ideas in this book and can be read in isolation from the rest of the text, like a "book within a book," or in conjunction with the chapters. It's up to you.

We learn, basically, by repetition. The most complex facts of life are really quite simple. This book is short; intentionally so. It is meant to be read over and over again, so that its basic truths will serve as meditations that you can look back on—and reflect on—over and over again until they become a regular part of your understanding of the world. Each time you read it, you will learn something new. You will take away from your reading whatever you are looking for at the time. This is a practical philosophy that you can and should use every day of your life.

SUCCESS IS NO ACCIDENT

SUCCESS IS NO ACCIDENT

Fig. 1. Horse Race

CHAPTER 1

THE DIFFERENCE THAT MAKES ALL THE DIFFERENCE

What do you think it takes to be a winner? Do you think successful people are born that way? Are you convinced they have higher IQs or know how to rub elbows with the right people? Or do you simply think that some people deserve success, while those who fail get what's coming to them? In this book, we're going to examine success and we're going to explain how you can become successful in whatever you choose to do.

People tend to confuse happiness with success. That confusion can send you looking in all the wrong places for success, and ultimately produce failure. You need to clarify and strengthen your understanding. So let's start here with a definition. It's the single meaning that applies to everyone:

Success is getting what you want.

This is not the same as being happy, which is enjoying what you already have. To be happy, you need nothing more. Just be satisfied with what you already have.

Successful people aren't all that different from those who never get what they want from life. And sometimes the difference between success and failure literally can be measured in inches. For example, look at Figure 1, showing the finish line of a horse race. The winner takes a prize of $15,000, while second place earns only $5,000. Does this mean that the winning horse is three times faster than the runner-up? Of course not! In fact, if we measure the difference between their running times and divide this by the total length of the racetrack, how much faster must the second-place horse run to beat the winner? Not much at all!

That's the way it is in life, too. People who earn three times more than others are not working three times harder. Nor do they have triple the knowledge, intelligence, or potential. They are simply more committed to achieving their goals and therefore are always finding opportunities that others fail to see.

Here's a story to illustrate my point. Two shoe salesmen were sent overseas to scout for new markets. Their first stop was a country where everyone was barefoot. The first salesman sent back a telegram to the home office saying: "Leaving tomorrow. No one wears shoes." The second salesman's telegram was very different. He said: "Great potential market. No competition." Remember, too, it's not just the big decisions you make in your life that determine your success. Little things, when you add them all up, make the big difference. Infinity is made up of seconds.

It's like the story about the man who told his friend that in order to avoid fights with his wife, he observes one rule: "Everything that's not important, my wife is the boss of, while in everything that is important, I am the boss."

"That's great," his friend replies. "No, it isn't," the man adds. "In the last forty years nothing important has happened!"

It is the commitment to always do your best—to work

hard and keep an open mind—even in the smallest things, that makes a tremendous difference in results. This is the difference that makes all the difference in every area of your life.

You may think that you already do your best, in every aspect of your life. But it is usually possible, if you make an extra effort to look with an open mind, to see even the most trivial problems in a different light. Here's a test to find out if you normally do your best when faced with a problem: Count the triangles in Figure 2. How many can you find? Be sure to count as many as you can. Most people fail to identify all the triangles. Answers vary from 10 to 150. To check the answer, see Figure 2A. Try to do it by yourself first, as this will demonstrate to you that no matter how good you are, you can always be better.

A simple answer like this shows us that it's always possible to do better. We normally operate at no more than 5 percent of our full mental capacity. Even Einstein probably used less than 10 percent of his intellectual abilities.

"But Einstein had the advantage of being born a genius," you say. That may be true. Some people really do start life with greater potential. However, if we normally use only 3 to 4 percent of our full mental capacities, we merely need to commit a fraction more of our resources to equal or even surpass the intelligence of people born with greater potential. If we compare the human brain to a computer, we see that it's not the hardware—or brain cells—that makes some people brighter than others. It's the software—the particular way of thinking—that differentiates the most successful people.

So the differences in success among people of similar ability result not from differences in their brains, but rather from

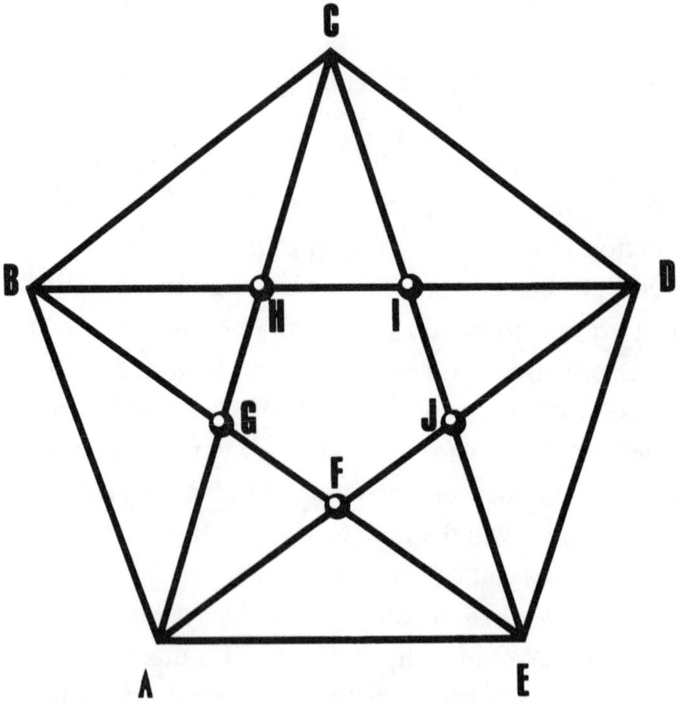

Fig. 2. Triangles

how well they have learned to use them. Success depends on strategy, not willpower. You can have the willpower to play basketball, but you will fail if you use a football strategy on a basketball court.

Competence—the ability to produce effective action in some domain—rather than having all the right answers, is what we need most in our lives. Why? Because just when we have all the answers, life changes the questions.

So it's not what you already know that counts, it's knowing how to acquire new information when you need it. If you suddenly forgot everything you ever learned in school, you'd still be better off than someone who'd never studied

In the figure there are 36 triangles:

- 10 singles (AGF, AGB, BGH, BHC, CHI, CID, DIJ, DJE, EJE, EFA)
- 10 doubles (AFB, BIC, CJD, DFE, EGA, AHB, BGC, CHD, DIE, EJA)
- 10 triples (ABE, ABC, BCD, CDE, AED, BIE, ACJ, BDF, CEG, ADH)
- 5 quintruples (ABD, BCE, CAD, DBE, ACE)
- 1 in the top part of the letter A

Fig. 2A. Answers

because during the study process you learned how to think. Learning how to think, not the facts we learn, is what's really important. Being able to apply ourselves to a problem creatively, and in the process notice opportunities where others don't, are crucial for achieving success. Anyone can learn to boost their mental capacity: You just have to know the right strategy.

For example, look at Figure 3. What do you see? At first glance, people often fail to pick out the Dalmatian. Check it out in Figure 3A. The dog in this illustration is like the opportunities in our lives: undoubtedly there, but visible only to the eye that's learned to look.

Only you can decide how to view a situation. The Chinese pictogram or symbol for crisis means both danger and opportunity. Most situations life presents are like that: The glass can either be half empty or half full. As the wisdom of the Chinese pictogram makes clear, even a crisis may present you with a positive opportunity.

You always have a choice in life.

Fig. 3. Dots

Your mind is so powerful that it can make your wishes come true. But often people don't learn to use their brains effectively. When you buy a household appliance, it comes with an owner's manual. But our mind—the most sophisticated "appliance" on earth—lacks an instruction booklet. We have to discover how to use it through trial and error, step by step. People who learn how to use their brains properly shoot ahead of the pack, while the others just mark time in the rear.

Just as you were able to see the Dalmatian in the picture once it was pointed out, you can also change the way you perceive the world. There are opportunities right there in your own life. They are obvious, but only to the prepared mind.

Fig. 3A. Dalmatian Dots

PRINCIPLE 1

Perceiving the Obvious

The difference that makes all the difference

The obvious is only obvious to the prepared mind.

The word "crisis" in Chinese has two meanings: danger and opportunity. A crisis situation has both possibilities. It is your mind that will decide which one to perceive.

It takes practice to learn to identify opportunity.

CHAPTER 2

THE SCIENCE OF SUCCESS

You may have some doubt at this point: Is it really possible to become successful so quickly and so easily?

Maybe not quickly—it takes time to learn and master the steps necessary for success. You have to apply yourself. But like physics or chemistry or any other academic subject, success can be taught and learned. If you study success systematically, you will become successful. The thing to remember is this:

Success is simple but not easy.

By reading this book attentively, you have already taken the first step toward success. You are already learning to use your mind in a different way. Having a prepared mind is one of the most important requirements for success.

Before I tell you what factors will contribute to your success, let's discuss a few of the things that stand in the way of success.

Consider this: If I asked you to walk across a plank that was laid out on the floor, you probably wouldn't refuse to walk on it. But if I were to place this same plank between the twin towers of the World Trade Center in New

York, you wouldn't take up this dare, even on a windless day with no glaring sunlight. How come? It's not that you can no longer physically walk across the plank, because the plank hasn't changed. But your head butts into the act, yelling: "Watch out! That's a lo-o-o-ng way to drop!" So you start to shake, stumble, and . . . whoops! This limitation on your performance is imposed by a negative message from your mind.

In the same way, negative programming instilled in us during our childhood gives us a false sense of limitation. If your mom was always telling you what a dumb kid you were, then you probably grew up believing you lacked the ability to learn. You may not have made it through to college. But this has nothing to do with your intelligence. Rather, you've been programmed to fail, so you expect to fail, and your expectations are fulfilled.

By the time you reach adulthood, your view of yourself is already set, much the way a thermostat controls the temperature of a room, keeping it at a constant pre-set level, regardless of what's happening outside. When the temperature in the room rises beyond the pre-set level, the air-conditioning switches on automatically. All of us have our own inner "thermostat," which we subconsciously use to fix our value as a person.

This principle applies to all areas of life. Take wealth, for example. All of us have a preconceived idea of how much we are "worth" in dollar terms. You might not be aware of it, but you project this figure into the world. It's almost as if you wear this number on your forehead. And this is precisely the value the world will hand you. If you don't think yourself worthy of being wealthy or well compensated for your work, your bank account will surely reflect those feelings. If you raise the level of your inner "thermostat," then the world around you will respond.

Remember that thermostat temperatures have nothing to do with the world outside. If the level is set to 68°F, then that's the temperature in the room, regardless of what's going on outside. If your inner "thermostat" reads half a million dollars, that's what the world will tend to channel your way, regardless of economic crises and doomsayers.

The world reflects the value you assign yourself.

You need to understand and let go of counterproductive tendencies—to reset your thermostat—in order to prepare for success.

As you expand your vision and change your perceptions by overcoming bad emotional programming, and by the many other insights and techniques that you will learn about later on in this book, you will realize that it is possible to create a new reality. Once you do so, success will surely come. It will only come, however, if you know exactly where your energies must be placed.

For success to be yours, you need three basic fundamentals to be working at the same time: *willingness, ability,* and *opportunity*. For example, let's say you want to win a big swimming race. You know how to swim, and you want to. But you can't swim without your goggles, which you don't have with you. Well, in that case, you've lost your opportunity.

Let's say you have your goggles, but you don't feel like swimming today. You can't win the race this way, either. Nor can you win the race if you are willing and even have your goggles, but do not know how to swim. Your success is going to depend on all three fundamentals being fully activated.

A simple but excellent stepping-stone to achievement is to be attentive to people who are already successful. Study them and try to identify and imitate their most effective habits. Through my own understanding of the world today, based both on my work as a doctor and researcher, and through my own experience lecturing on success around the world, I have learned the fundamentals of the science of success. My goal is to teach them to you.

Success is a science that has discrete components.

The science of success is made up of various components. As you learn and develop them, your mind expands, your intelligence soars, and your capacity to cope with routine problems improves. Like points on a star, these components are all equally important, as they support each other. You can't shift one without affecting the others.

PRINCIPLE 2

Physical Manifestation

The mind as co-creator

Everything in the physical universe appears first in the mind. Thought is energy, and energy follows thought.

Thoughts spur feelings that generate behavior. Behavior prompts consequences in the physical universe that will in turn trigger new thoughts, completing the think-feel-act cycle.

Individual thoughts depend on the beliefs of the thinker. If you dislike what's happening in your physical universe, analyze what you've been thinking and what beliefs lie behind your thoughts. Change your beliefs and new opportunities will appear in your life.

CHAPTER 3

THE WORLD OF ILLUSIONS

What is real? It seems to be an easy question to answer. Since our sensory organs feed us information so that we can get an accurate sense of the world around us, what we see with our own eyes, hear with our own ears, touch with our own hands, smell with our nose, taste with our tongue are all real. Nonetheless, our senses are not foolproof. Sometimes they mislead us, giving us a false sense of reality. Judging by our senses alone, if we were asked, we'd have to say that the Earth stands still. Yet we know it is really spinning at an incredible speed. Just by looking, we'd probably say the Earth is flat, but we know it is spherical. So what *seems* real is not always so.

Keep that in mind, because one of our greatest mistakes is to rely entirely on our senses. It's very hard not to believe what you see with your own eyes. Look at Figure 4: Which silhouette is the tallest? They're all exactly the same size—check with a ruler if you like. You think you see a difference in size because of the way your mind interprets this drawing. The apparent variation in size is nothing more than a visual illusion, caused by the brain's different interpretation of the same visual phenomena.

So be careful of making judgments in life based on what

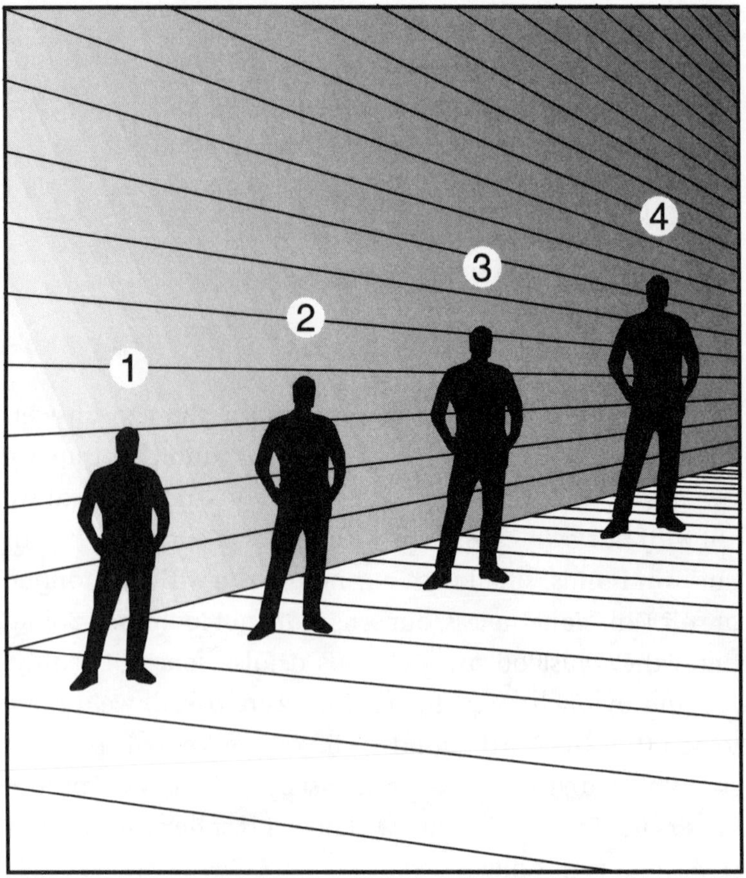

Fig. 4. Silhouettes

seems obvious. We often hear people say things like, "I'm sure he's a crook. I know his type." Your opinion may result from an unconscious assumption dating back to childhood. For example, if some mustachioed neighbor had a fight with your father way back when you were a little kid, any new acquaintance with a mustache may evoke long-buried memories without your even being aware of it.

Another mistake we often make by relying on our senses is thinking that what is now always is. In Figure 5, we see a series of black squares separated by white spaces. Sometimes when we look at it, we see the strips of white lines intersecting each other; other times the black squares dominate. But sometimes, between those black squares hover a few gray dots. Are they also real? That depends—when we see them, they are; when we don't see them, they're not. It's like reality itself—always dynamic, always changing.

In our own lives we think things never change. We say to ourselves, I know my husband very well; we've been married for fifteen years. Maybe you've been married to a man named Joe, but the Joe you married back then is not the same man today. So, too, you can never step in the same river twice. You put your foot in once, but it's not the same when you dip it in again.

We act as though we are the same and treat others as though they haven't changed, either. This turns out to be a great handicap in life because if we don't see how we are changing, we may be operating out of outmoded ideas and fall behind.

Leave room for people—and things—to alter. Including yourself. Likewise, do not think that everything you see, know, and assume is an indisputable fact.

It's like the old story. A man is invited to the home of a young lady he is dating for the first time. She is frying ham. He notices that she keeps cutting off the edge and throwing it away. "But why do you keep cutting off the

Fig. 5. Black Squares

edge?" he asks her. "Because my mother did it that way." The young man, perplexed by this, goes to the young lady's mother and observes her as she, too, cuts off the edges of the ham to fry it. He asks her the same question, and she gives him the same reply: "Because my mother did it."

Finally, he goes to the grandmother and asks her the same question, and she replies, "I had to cut the ham, the pan was too small."

Don't just keep doing things the way they were done before. Question your convictions. You must leave room for people—and things—to alter. And that includes you. Today you're probably quite different from the way you were five or ten years ago.

Another error lies in thinking that what's on the surface is all there is. Figure 6 depicts a truck with a blowout carrying a cargo of tires. Is there anything inherently funny about a truck transporting a load of tires? No. Is a truck with a flat tire really amusing? Again, no. There is no humor in any one element of the picture. But once our brains put these elements together—a truck with a flat carrying a full load of tires—our minds create humor out of the relationship it finds between these two facts. The picture illustrates a real situation, but it is necessary to incorporate an abstract concept (the paradox inherent in the situation) for us to obtain a more complete reading of the reality depicted.

The whole world is full of such pitfalls. How many opportunities do we miss by believing that what we *think* is real is? By believing that nothing changes? "Reality" is subjective. Some people may think this book is fantastic; others will say it's a waste of time. They are both right. The book is not objectively good or bad. Those who are open to its message will find it spectacular. For others, it will fall on deaf ears.

Our minds are constantly creating our own reality. In the same way, we can create success in our own lives.

The map is not the territory.

Fig. 6. Truckload

PRINCIPLE 3

Learning with the Universe

The greatest of all teachers is the universe itself. The universe is pure intelligence, well ordered, ruled by immutable sovereign laws. These laws are absolute in their essence, interdependent in their applicability, independent of the time and space where they operate, and dependent on the divine awareness and intention present in each of us.

Their purpose is to maintain order within chaos, love within hate, wisdom within ignorance, health in sickness, and eternity in the most fleeting moment.

Each principle in this book incorporates and reflects one of these laws. If you can incorporate the laws of the universe into your psychological structure—by being aware of them, internalizing them, and practicing them in your daily life—success and wisdom will surely follow.

CHAPTER 4

LIKING YOURSELF MORE

Self-esteem is crucial to success in every area of life. If you don't like yourself, how can you expect others to like you?

Self-esteem problems often begin in childhood, when parents unwittingly convey negative and limiting messages to their impressionable kids. In the years from birth to seven, the brain acts like a sponge, absorbing everything unquestioningly, conscious but unaware, and lacking cognitive capacities. If you are taught during this period that money is the root of all evil, or that rich people never go to heaven, the messages will penetrate deep into your unconscious. You'll probably never get rich when you grow up—and you'll never understand why.

If you listen carefully to what teachers and parents say to three- and four-year-olds most of the time, you will notice that the kids are reprimanded much more than complimented. This difference can be as much as one hundred fold. It's no wonder that our infant selves, bombarded with these negative messages, begin to set limits on what we attempt to do.

This is not much different from training fleas. Don't laugh. It's true. Do you know how to train a flea? Put it in a jar and close the lid. Immediately, it begins to jump. Every time it flies up, it hits the lid and drops back to the bottom of the jar. After a few repetitions, it realizes that there's no point to jumping so high, and its hops become less powerful, not hitting the lid anymore. Once this stage of self-limitation has been reached, you can take the lid away and the flea will never jump out. Its mind has conditioned its efforts to a certain "ceiling," and it will never again check to see if the lid is really still there.

We humans are just like the flea. Our parents' early messages are the "lids" that limit our thinking—and we are generally unaware of them.

As we grow up, we gradually manage to throw off some of those lids. But how many more remain imperceptible? How many were hammered into us day after day by those thousands of "don'ts" of our childhood? How many "don'ts" still persist, your adult need for them still unappraised, their real importance for your present and future life unknown?

You can reverse this negative way of viewing yourself at any age, provided you realize that you are capable of learning and achieving a great deal more than you know today. Starting today, you can change your life for the better and get on the road to success. No one can make you feel inferior unless you let them. It's your own choice. If someone makes you feel belittled or unhappy, it's because you let them. Only you can decide what to feel.

To get a better idea of why it's so hard to change these deeply ingrained beliefs, look at Figure 7. It shows a ship about to hit a large iceberg, most of which is concealed beneath the water. It's the size of the underwater section that makes the iceberg so dangerous to the ship. If it were just a matter of hitting a chunk of ice the size of the exposed

Fig. 7. Iceberg and Ship

portion, the ship would have a much better chance of dislodging the ice and surviving the crash.

Think of your mind as an iceberg. The vast majority of

what you think goes on "below water," unseen and inaccessible to you. It is in this powerful underwater section, called "the unconscious," that the messages of childhood are buried. Trying to dislodge them is not easy. You can't do it rationally, by simply telling yourself those messages you heard about being dumb or fat just aren't true. And yet this is what education in Western societies encourages us to do, with its emphasis on developing the rational left hemisphere of the brain. But in order to change yourself you must reach to your unconscious mind through the right hemisphere, which is the gateway to the unconscious. The strengths of each side of the brain will be discussed in greater detail in Chapter 8.

There's a special force within you waiting to be released. You just have to learn how to tap into it. There are a number of well-supported scientific reports on people acquiring superhuman strength under extreme stress. One of the most famous cases is that of a small woman who was able to lift the body of a car weighing several tons high enough to pull out her four-year-old child, who had become trapped under the car when her jack slipped. How did she manage to do this? Where did this inner strength come from? Certainly not from her muscles. It came from her unconscious. Do you doubt that you can erase the errors of your childhood and learn to be successful by reading this book? It sounds strange, I know. New knowledge often seems unbelievable or even magical when it is first discovered.

Let positive experiences replace negative input to boost your self-esteem.

In the same way it seems hard to understand how, given the negative messages pounded into your unconscious in childhood, you can do anything.

But there are new approaches to the problem that have had very good results. Imagine for a minute that your mind is a jar filled with different-shaped candies. Let's assume that the half-moon candies correspond to the negative messages assimilated during childhood—"I'm dumb," "I'm ugly," "I can't do anything right," "nobody likes me"—all those downers that slipped in when you weren't looking.

Obviously you would like to eliminate those half-moon candies, or negative feelings. One way would be to pick them out one by one and throw them away. But this would take a long time, as some negative feelings are unconscious and we do not even know they exist. This is the route of traditional Freudian-based psychology.

Another, more effective way to get rid of negative feelings is to cram in more positive ones. Forcing in more positive messages will force the negative messages—or half-moon candies—out. By gradually replacing the negative messages with positive ones, you can boost your self-esteem considerably (this will be discussed in the next chapter). And when you feel better about yourself, the entire world improves.

When you change, the world changes with you.

PRINCIPLE 4

The Universal Paradox

Accepting the unacceptable

In life, you are what you refuse to be. If you declare, "I don't want to be like my mother," then you'll surely grow to resemble her—and everyone except you will be acutely aware of this.

The wisdom of self-acceptance is a concept found in all religions and philosophies. A real change will only take place within you if you accept yourself the way you are and accept others the way they are.

CHAPTER 5

RE-CREATING YOURSELF

The universe is paradoxical. You only have credit when you don't need money. Only when you accept yourself can you change.

Your behavior tends to follow the path of least resistance. If you believe you are incompetent, that's your path of least resistance. Therefore you will be more prone to fail. The way to change this is through the unconscious. Its pathway is in the right brain. Most of our training, though, is to approach problems using our left brain.

Here's a story that illustrates my point: A man was looking for his lost wallet. "What are you doing?" asked his friend. "I'm looking for my wallet," he answered. "Well, where did you lose it?" his friend continued. "Over there," he replied. "Then why are you looking here?" "Because this is where the light is."

It's the same with people who are trying to solve all their problems using only their left brain. It just doesn't work because the problem isn't located there.

Here are some techniques—outlined in the book *See You at the Top* by Zig Ziglar—that you can use to develop your right-brain capabilities. They will help you tap into your creative potential, increasing your chances for success.

- **Relaxation.** At school you were taught that hard work is good for you; it builds your character. Sure, up to a point. But this is only true when you also know how to relax and slip your brain into the alpha mode. This mode, which can be measured by electrodes placed on your head, is also known as the *accelerated learning mode* and is identified when the body is relaxed but the mind is alert, allowing for greater creativity. There are many relaxation techniques—deep breathing, special music, meditation, yoga, and so on—to help relieve harmful stress.

  Not all stress, by the way, is harmful. A certain amount is good, spurring us on to achievement or helping us to channel our energies.

- **Visualization.** Visualization is a crucial tool for installing experiences in the nervous system. If you visualize something really well, your mind cannot distinguish between the real thing and your imagination. Picture what you want—include all the details. Make it as real as possible.

  A research project carried out at an American university dramatizes the effectiveness of visualization. Thirty students were selected to test their aim on a firing range. None of them had ever fired a gun before. A short list was drawn up of all those with the same average score. They were then split into three groups. The first group trained with real guns for twenty minutes a day, five days a week, for six weeks. The second group followed the same schedule as the first, but merely visualized firing using nothing more than a cocked finger. The third group also went to the firing range, but just fooled around. After six weeks the tests were repeated. The first group improved 83 percent. The second group improved 82 percent. The third group scored the same as they had on first try. This test showed that the gun is nothing more than a means to train and concentrate the mind—the hand and the eye, too.

- **Accepting failure.** How did we all learn to walk? By falling down and getting up again, over and over, until we got it right. If at some point in your training you had remained on the ground, thinking, "No way I'll ever get this right; I guess I'll just stay right here!" you wouldn't be walking around today. But babies haven't been programmed yet—they go on trying and failing until one day they get it right and actually manage to toddle a few steps. Our education teaches us that failure is synonymous with sin—and gradually our self-esteem gets worn away.

  Mistakes can be the turning points of our lives. There's nothing really important in life that you get right the first time around. If you say, "I don't want to make mistakes," it will be harder to forge ahead in life. The more you accept your failures, the more you learn from them, and the better your chances of getting it right next time. As you get better at something through practice, you become freer and more confident, and your self-esteem blossoms.

- **Smile.** Did you know there is a direct connection between your smile and your central nervous system? When you smile, even if you don't feel particularly cheerful, your mind gets a message that everything's fine. Every smile releases a hormone called beta-endorphine, which transmits a positive message to your brain.

  Did you know that women smile far more than men?

Several studies have proved this. And as you probably know, women live an average eight years longer than men. Do their smiles have anything to do with this? You bet they do!

In a study carried out in a psychiatric hospital, two groups of depressed patients were treated with the same course of medicines. One group had their mouths held in a smiling position by tape. This group improved far faster than the other group because their smiles—even though involuntary—transmitted a happy message to their brains.

In a recent experiment, a group of Japanese people, who are culturally conditioned to smile at their neighbors, watched a horror movie while being monitored for stress hormones. First they watched the horror movie together, occasionally glancing at their companions and smiling. They then watched the movie in isolation, with no one to smile at. The first situation produced slower heartbeats and far lower levels of catecolamines (a mixture of adrenaline and noradrenaline hormones), proving that smiling slows stress hormone output.

Give of yourself. Give to a loved one, a friend, or to your community. Do something for nothing, and you will soon find that the world turns your offering back to you in another form.

Surround yourself with positive people. It's hard to develop self-esteem if you live with negative people. This doesn't necessarily mean you must cast off people who need you. But you must pick places and relationships that further your own well-being. If you don't feel good about yourself, you can never help others feel better—a vicious cycle that may be harmful to all involved.

- **Concentrate on your strengths.** We're often told to work on our weak points. That's all wrong. What we should do is concentrate on our abilities. Work on your strong points, and the rest will follow. Figure 8 shows a pro basketball player, alongside a professional jockey. Imagine the basketball pro tying to be a jockey. Pity the poor horse—it might never make it out of the starting gate! And can you see the jockey trying to slam-dunk a basketball? In life you find a lot of jockeys trying to play pro basketball, and a lot of basketball players trying to race thoroughbreds. They spend all their lives struggling with their liabilities and ignoring the potential of their assets.

  What you have to do is find out what your assets are and concentrate on developing them. The moment you do so, your liabilities begin to disappear. How? By being committed to using these assets, setting new goals based on them, and achieving these goals. As you fully utilize your assets, you will be less concerned with your liabilities. Do an inventory: What are my assets and how can I develop them even more?

Success goes to the successful.
Love to those who have love.

Like attracts like. From the lake to the river, and from the river to the sea, water flows to water. Money flows to people with money, not to the poor. Success to the successful. Love to the lover. Hatred to the bitter.

Think about your best friend for a moment. How many things do you have in common?

Link yourself to your past successes—professional,

Fig. 8. Jockey and Basketball Player

romantic, personal, or spiritual. The important point is the experience of success—and to firm up the mind-set that brought this success. Visualize this success in your present life, and you will attract success for the future. Success attracts success; but only you can start the process.

PRINCIPLE 5

Attraction in Action

Wherever your attention is concentrated, that's where your energy flows. Like attracts like. You can only attract what you already have.

Life is an echo. If you don't like what you're getting, check what you're giving out.

CHAPTER 6

YOU MUST BELIEVE BEFORE YOU SEE

Almost a century ago a leading philosopher and psychologist, the Harvard professor William James, was asked to name the most important discovery in the field of human development over the past hundred years. "The bird doesn't sing because it's happy; it's happy because it sings," he surprisingly replied. Then he explained what he meant: "Until now, it was always thought that it was necessary to feel in order to act. But now we know that if we act, the feeling follows. I believe this is the most important discovery of the century for human development."

Doubting Thomas said that seeing is believing. But he got things the wrong way around. We must first believe in order to see (Figure 9). If you wait to see before you believe, you'll always be a runner-up, trailing along behind people who believed and—armed with their belief—managed to see.

Everything depends upon belief. Belief creates opportunity. If you believe you will fail, you won't even begin to try. But if you try, there is always a chance you will succeed. If you fail, you can always try again. With belief the possibilities are endless.

Most people say, "I'll do it the moment I feel like it."

Fig. 9. Believing Is Seeing

That's not the way successful people operate. People who succeed start to do things right away and then find that soon after they can feel the effects of their efforts.

Believing is seeing instead of seeing is believing.

Behavior changes feelings; feelings change through behavior. Intention without action is a delusion. Belief directs action, which directs results.

True belief is the belief in possibility. It is very critical to be able to distinguish between possibility and expectation. Everything I plan in my future I plan as a possibility. If it doesn't happen, it continues to be a possibility. If I plan my future as an expectation, I will become frustrated if it doesn't work out; I will lose my ability to believe.

Expectations destroy belief. Possibilities allow infinite belief.

A person will say, "You don't understand, I've got so many problems . . ." "How can I believe enough to try something new when everything and everyone have disappointed me . . . ?" "You have no idea of the difficulties in my life . . ." "It's easy for you to dream up smart sayings about life and success, because you don't have to cope with my problems."

Plenty of people feel like this, seeing the way ahead blocked by the problems they have to face. Life is really just one hassle after another.

But listen to this: Problems are good for you! The moment something becomes a problem, it means you can do something about it. It's a sign to you that you have the opportunity to excel.

Every problem has within it the seed of its solution.

Here's a story from my life that taught me this powerful lesson: When I was twelve years old, living in Juiz de Fora, a little town in the interior of Brazil, our neighbor's dog disappeared. The neighbor claimed to the local policeman, who wasn't very smart, that I'd stolen the dog; meanwhile, I didn't even know she had a pet. She pressed charges against me and I was summoned to the precinct. I begged my father to go with me, but he refused, telling me I should handle my own problems. I had to get my uncle to go with me.

At the precinct, the officer accused me of stealing the dog.

"You took it!"

"I didn't!"

"You did!"

"I did not!"

The argument stretched on until I was called impertinent for answering back. The policeman finally decided I was guilty and issued a fine.

My father refused to help me so I had no idea how to pay. But I had earned some pocket money tutoring classmates who'd failed their year-end examinations. It was exactly the amount of the fine. So I had to use the first money I ever earned to pay a fine that was probably nonexistent under law, for something I hadn't done. For many years afterward I felt my father had been overly harsh and I resented him.

Later, as unfair as the situation may have been, I realized that there was a positive side to it. I learned at an early age that I had to rely on myself to resolve my problems. This led me to see most things in life in a different light. Since the age of twelve, I have never asked anybody for anything. By the time I was nineteen, I was already financially independent.

This phenomenon is echoed in nature. A Nobel Prize–winning scientist, Ilya Prigogine, described the world as operating within two different systems: a closed system, having entropy with the universe, and an open system, having syntropy with the universe. A car or a house or anything that has the potential to get worn down, becomes useless, and that which cannot renew itself is a closed system. *Entropy,* in other words, is a state of deterioration or disintegration. On the other hand, in open systems, there is constant renewal, evolution, or *syntropy*. The individual and society are capable of learning and therefore of evolving. The human brain and civilization are syntropic, or open systems.

In an open system, when you pose a problem, the system will either disintegrate under the effects of that problem or it will grow. So, for example, if you take a person from a small town and drop him in the middle of a big city, he will either become a psychiatric patient and fall apart or he will become a citizen of the city and thrive.

Our lives are an open system. Whenever we have a problem, it means we are being presented with the possibility of growing. How we handle each problem and what we learn from it are what count. As soon as you begin to learn from your difficulties, life gets better. This is why I often say to people lamenting their lot in life, our problems are our best friends.

All problems bear within them the seeds of their solutions. A problem crops up in your life only if you have the power to solve it or in some way contribute to its solution. A beggar does not have any problems with the destruction of the Amazon rain forest, because he's more worried about where his next meal is coming from.

If there were no problems for you to resolve at work, you'd be out of a job. They wouldn't need you any more.

The only place where there are no more problems is in the cemetery. No one there has to cope with any problems at all. But if you're alive, it means you'll be coping with one crisis after another. When you are successful, not only can you solve your problems, but you can look forward to rising to the challenge.

PRINCIPLE 6

Abundance

It all depends on your point of view

The universe is potentially abundant, created for everyone to have his or her fill. When Jack wins, Jill doesn't necessarily lose, unless she really makes a point of it—but that's her decision, and her problem.

Your beliefs will shape your perceptions. Abundance is a universal right. Hunger and poverty are not in keeping with nature. Suffering is a manifestation of being out of step with oneself and the laws of the universe. Abundance or scarcity, grief or joy, basically depend on individual choice or perception.

CHAPTER 7

GETTING RID OF NEGATIVITY

Some people think they're the greatest, that they can do no wrong. That's called having delusions of grandeur. Depending on whether they have the ability to back up their high opinions, they may or may not be successful. Other people can't find a good thing to say about themselves; they believe they can't do anything right. They have delusions of negativity. And no matter how they try, they're surely not successful.

Positive thinking is not the same thing as delusions of grandeur. With positive thinking, you have a goal in mind that you haven't yet achieved. With delusions of grandeur, you are not in touch with reality and believe that you have achieved your objective without actually having done so. Positive thinking alone doesn't help; but on the other hand, negative thinking hinders.

Do you recognize any of the following destructive thoughts? If so, get rid of them. They're standing in the way of your progress.

1. **If at first you don't succeed, you are a failure.**
   There is no such thing as failure; there is only feedback. If you only did things that you did well from the beginning, you wouldn't be able to do anything at all!

2. **If I am deterred from my goal, even for a short time, I might as well give up.**

   Nothing you aim to do in life will follow a straight course. You cannot predict what will happen; you can only be open to all possibilities.

3. **I am a victim of circumstances (because of my husband, my wife, my mother, and so on). I'm not in charge of my life. There is always someone else who has power, not me.**

   You must take full responsibility for yourself: You must realize that you are the only one who can truly alter the circumstances of your life. Take full charge of your life, otherwise you will never have the authority it takes to be a success.

4. **Work is something we must tolerate until vacation comes.**

   If this is the way you think, it means that 50 percent of your waking life is unhappy; because that's the percentage of your life you spend working. That's giving up too much. You have the ability to enjoy what you do, if only you make the commitment to put your heart and mind into it. There is no such thing as a good or bad project—it's you who determines that. If you decide to go ahead with a project, then it is a good project.

5. **You are either lucky or not lucky.**

   This is utter nonsense. Luck happens when preparation meets opportunity. Luck is relative. A lot depends on how you perceive a situation.

   This reminds me of a story. There once was a poor boy who lived in China. Seated on the sidewalk outside his house one day, he dreamed of owning a horse but lacked the money to buy one. Just then the cavalry passed by, accompanied by a colt that was unable to keep pace. Aware of the lad's dearest wish, the leader of the troop gave him the colt. A neighbor commented to the boy's father, "Your son's really lucky!"

"How come?" asked the father.

"Because he wanted a horse, the cavalry rides by, and he's given a colt. Isn't that luck?"

"Might be good luck, might be bad luck," retorted the boy's father. "Only time will tell. . . ."

You haven't won or lost until you've removed the chips from the table.

The boy cared lovingly for the colt, but one day it ran away. This time the neighbor said, "Gee, your son's unlucky. He was given a colt, took care of it, and now that it's full-grown it runs away. Isn't that bad luck?"

"Might be good luck, might be bad luck," retorted the boy's father once again. "Only time will tell. . . ."

Awhile later the horse reappeared, bringing with it a herd of wild horses. The neighbor commented once again, "Gee, your son's lucky. His horse ran away, but now it has come back with a herd of wild horses, which all belong to him."

The father replied once again, "Might be good luck, might be bad luck. Only time will tell. . . ."

One day the boy was breaking one of the horses in when he fell off and fractured his leg. Once again the neighbor commented, "Gee, your son's unlucky. That horse ran away, came back with a whole herd of wild horses, and now the kid breaks his leg training one of them."

"Might be good luck, might be bad luck," retorted the boy's father yet again. "Only time will tell. . . ."

A few days later, the ruler of this realm declared war on a rival kingdom. All the young men were called up to fight except the lad with the broken leg. And the neighbor started off again, "Gee, your son's lucky. . . ."

That's how it is in life: Things may be lucky or unlucky. It all depends on what happens afterward. What seems like a bad break may later turn out to have been your lucky day.

6. **Only when somebody starts giving me what I need will I give to them.**

The universe always gives back to you what you give. If you give to one person you may not get anything back from them directly, but someone or something else surely will.

PRINCIPLE 7

Unity without Complexity

One for all and all for one

We're all part of the Gestalt energy called the universe: Infinite, God, the Source, the All or Whole. Everything we think, say, or do contributes positively or negatively to this All.

If your life is plagued by fears and disharmony, you made a negative contribution to the universal vibration.

On the other hand if you live harmoniously, respecting your relationship with your fellow beings, you are fostering universal success.

CHAPTER 8

SEEING THE FOREST *AND* THE TREES

Few people realize how much success depends upon the ability to balance the different kinds of thinking processes we are capable of. You might assume that the skilled accountant who can add up columns of figures in his head or the brilliant painter who creates great works of art is destined for success. But that's not necessarily so. The accountant, who has great strength in logical, meticulous, objective thinking, may never get beyond being a backroom bookkeeper. The brilliant painter is intuitive and carefree in her thinking, but she lies in bed unemployed and depressed; all her works are stuffed into the closet.

Each person has greater strength in a different side of the brain: The accountant has a stronger left brain; the painter a stronger right brain. Each suffers for lack of what the other has.

All of us think and perceive through the two hemispheres into which our brains are divided, each of which governs different ways of thinking. Take a look at the picture in Figure 10. If I ask the logical left brain what is in this picture, the left brain will see it as a bunch of squiggles. But the intuitive right brain will see a whole orchestra and its conductor. The left sees details, but cannot see the whole

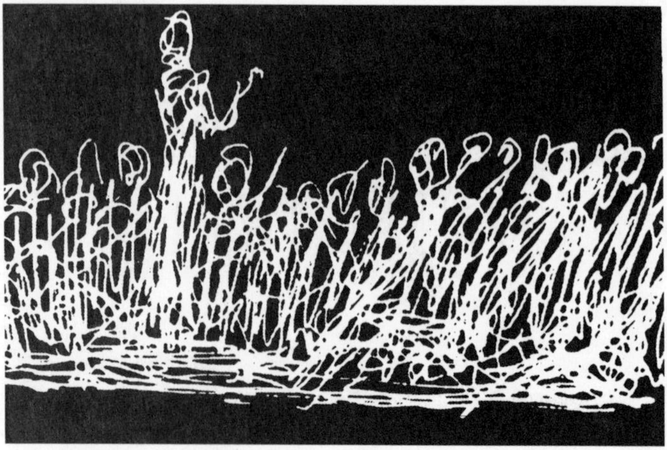

Fig. 10. Squiggles/Orchestra

picture. The right sees the whole picture, but does not pay attention to the details. The difference is the right hemisphere finds sense in what the left dismisses as nonsense.

Generally speaking, the left side of our brain governs logic and the right side creativity. Each side processes information in different—but complementary—ways, expanding our capacity for comprehending the world and acting effectively within it. The list in Figure 11 identifies more of these specific differences.

To succeed in life we need the abilities of each of these cerebral hemispheres to be in balance. We must be able to work with both sides of our brain. Unfortunately, for reasons that I will explain, most of us do not know or have not yet learned to do this.

We who live in Western societies, which generally emphasize development of the logical and sequential left half of the brain, tend to value the banker more than the

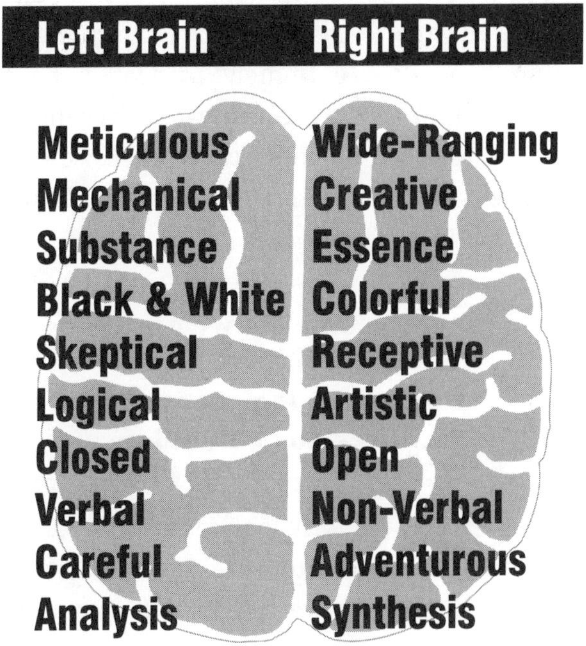

Fig. 11. List of Left/Right Sides of the Brain

artist. And because so much of our life takes place on an unconscious level, which cannot be reached through this logical left side, our left brain, worshipping society, misses or fails to resolve problems that can only be solved through the more intuitive, free-associating right brain.

Think of how you feel when you get stuck working out a problem. You think and you think, but you get nowhere; then suddenly, when you're not actively thinking about the problem—you may be half asleep—the answer seems to come to you out of the blue. That's the right brain at work.

Did you know that some of the greatest discoveries in history were made, not in a moment of intense concentration but in a moment of relaxation? Thomas Edison tried many different ways to create incandescent light. He tested everything. One day, extremely frustrated, he thought maybe the solution to the problem was somewhere else. As he began to doze off, he came up with his solution. And Albert Einstein made his observations about relativity while he was resting in a hammock.

To succeed in life we need the abilities of both sides of the brain—the logical and the creative—to be in balance.

In my work I particularly look for techniques to develop the right brain. It is crucial to have a balance. The moment you create a conflict between your left and right brain, everything gets thrown off; your immune system gets depressed and you feel confused. Your left brain may say, "I'm going to cheat on my husband/wife," while your right brain says, "Don't do it." The argument between them can undermine both your integrity and your health.

The left brain sees the trees but not the forest. It can identify the details of a project but not visualize it as a complete whole. The right brain sees the forest but not the trees. It has the big picture but not enough of the details.

To be really successful in life, you have to build a bridge from one hemisphere to the other. When you do, you actually make changes in your brain chemistry. Compensating for weaknesses in either side of your brain, you increase your ability to make connections and switches. The total effect of having both sides in balance is greater than the sum of the parts. Not only will it increase your IQ and boost your self-esteem, it will help you succeed on every level of your life.

PRINCIPLE 8

Cognitive Dissonance

Antagonistic forces generate conflict

Inner conflicts occur when two opposing beliefs come together within the same individual or when people act in ways that run counter to their own beliefs. Such inner conflicts drain vital energies.

When conflicts like this occur, people try to minimize the differences by altering one of the sides. For example, if you think smoking is bad for you but light up nevertheless, you create a conflict between belief and action. If you deal with this split by trying to fool yourself into thinking that smoking isn't so bad for you after all, you're rationalizing. When rationalization is the major way of dealing with inner conflict, you are living in a state of self-delusion.

CHAPTER 9

COMMUNICATING POSITIVELY WITH YOURSELF

One of the most important secrets you can learn in life is that the way you communicate with yourself and others determines what happens in your life. Language creates reality. Henry Ford said, "If you think you can, or you think you can't, you're right either way." Whether you say the glass is half empty or half full, that answer becomes the truth. Though both interpretations are accurate, the language you use to describe it says that you either "have" or "don't have."

This concept that language creates reality is one of the basic tenets of neuro-linguistic programming (known as NLP for short). NLP, which uses language to change mental programs, can achieve outstanding results very fast: It focuses on the process rather than the content. This technique can help you train your mind to pinpoint opportunities. The basic concept of neuro-linguistic programming is present throughout this book and can contribute greatly to your success.

Communication is one of the most primary human needs. Poor communication with yourself can cost you success, happiness, and prosperity. Crossed lines of communication with family and friends strain love and intimacy.

Scrambled communications in the workplace waste money. At school, weak communication can jeopardize the future of our children. Many undesirable things can be avoided if we only communicate more effectively.

Let's start with inner communication: Your communication with yourself. Your language is composed of patterns of recurring conversations you have with yourself: "I always make the same mistake . . ." "How did I get into this mess again . . . ?" "I don't know enough to succeed." On and on it goes. Unless you analyze your own destructive thought and speech patterns, and try to break them, you will keep repeating the same thing over and over again. Once you control this self-talk, you can control your life.

Language not only explains reality, it also creates it. Our emotions live in our explanations of things, not in the thing itself. If someone says "I am unhappy because my husband keeps losing his job," that would not be entirely correct. You can be sorry about his situation, but it is not the source of your unhappiness. You choose to explain whatever unhappiness you feel, using this as the cause. But if you change the explanation, you change the emotion.

This also explains a lot about the real source of low self-esteem. When you see how much of your life is determined by the language you use, you will discover that every assessment you make of yourself is a prediction of your behavior. If you decide that you are able to explain something, your behavior toward explaining it will be quite different than if you decide that you cannot.

The language you use is of prime importance to achieving your goals. Unfortunately, over 95 percent of the world's population takes a negative approach. Our minds are attuned to a *negative* discourse. Most of us were trained to focus more on what we don't like than on what we really want. For example, instead of saying, "I want to be successful," we may say, "I don't want to fail"; instead of saying, "I want to be slim," we say, "I don't want to be fat." The unconscious goes right to the heart of the matter. So when you say, "I don't want to be fat," it latches onto "want to be fat." If you say, for example, "Don't think about the color red!" is it possible to think of any other color?

The same thing occurs when you say, "I don't want to fail." Your subconscious hears the word "fail" and you do everything to guarantee your failure without realizing it.

Every assessment you make of yourself is a prediction of your behavior.

Focusing on what you don't want, instead of what you do want, is like driving while looking only in the rearview mirror. You know where you're coming from, but you don't know where you're going! So, one way to upgrade our existence on this planet is to learn to use more appropriate language when we talk to ourselves through that little voice deep inside us all. What voice?

That one—the voice that's asking you, "What voice?"

By remodeling our communications with ourselves, we can change our inner representation—and our emotional condition.

Treat yourself like your best friend.

PRINCIPLE 9

Transcendence and Freedom of Choice

Choosing to be free

Through proper use of the mind, we can mitigate or transcend events predetermined by circumstancial forces. Transcendence means rising above and starting over.

It is always possible to choose how you react to events. Those who let themselves be carried along by circumstances become part of the problem. By self-observation and acts of integrity and compassion, you can develop the ability to give a positive connotation to an unpleasant event as soon as it occurs.

We are linguistic animals and thus have the capacity to transcend at any time. If freedom of choice did not allow us this transcendence, everything would be incoherent, a cosmic mess.

CHAPTER 10

COMMUNICATING WITH THE WORLD

Sir Francis Bacon once said that knowledge is power. Personally, I don't find this altogether correct. Knowledge is power only when it's put into action. What's the value of a person equipped with a vast storehouse of knowledge, who learns whole encyclopedias by heart, but who cannot communicate with others? Zero!

There are four ways in which you communicate with the world, all of which affect the way people judge you:

- What you do and how you talk about it
- How you look
- What you say
- How you say it

Let's start with what you do and how you talk about it.

There is a story about two bricklayers working on building the Notre Dame Cathedral in Paris. When each man was asked what he was doing, the first one said, "My job is putting one brick on top of another." Whereas the second one said, "I am creating a monument to the glory of God!"

What you communicate to others about your work tells them how to think about you.

You also tell others a lot by the way you look and behave. If you don't look like the owner of your own life, your life will look like it's been stolen. If you don't act like you can fly a plane, no one will fly with you, even if you're a terrific pilot. You have to walk your talk.

The power of what you communicate by how you look is monumental. Researchers performed an experiment to test the effect of outward appearance on others. They hired several college students to stand at the entrance of a subway and told them to solicit money by telling people that they had forgotten their wallets and couldn't buy a token. They asked each person for money for the fare. In one hour they each got around six dollars. During the second hour, they each put on a tie and nearly tripled their take. Now you might be thinking they got more money because they were more practiced in asking. The researchers were aware of that factor, too. So, the following day, the students returned to the subway and did the same thing in reverse. This time they wore the tie first and removed it for the second hour. Again, they got three time as much money when they wore the tie.

Suitability matters, too. If you want to play for the Mets, you don't sport a Dodgers cap. You have to look your part.

You have only one chance to make a good first impression. Opinions about other people tend to be based on the first three or four minutes of a first meeting. And this image can last for twenty years.

Walk your talk!

A number of years ago an experiment was done to show just how powerful those first impressions can be for communicating who you are to other people. A group of executives who didn't know each other were invited to a cocktail party. After fifteen minutes the party was halted. Everyone took a piece of paper, wrote down the names of the people they had met, and gave them a grade from 1 to 10 indicating what they thought about each person. Over the following six months they all then got to know each other. At the end of that period they were all invited back to another party and were asked again to give each person a grade. They discovered that there was no difference between the grade they gave after six months and the grade they gave after fifteen minutes.

You don't get a second chance to make a good first impression.

To communicate effectively to others you must communicate completely. What do I mean by that? Well, for one thing, how you speak is just as important as the content. In fact, it can determine the content. The way you say things can change the meaning. One sentence can have many different meanings depending on where you place the emphasis. Follow this little workout:

Sentence: *I didn't say he stole that money*!

Now read this sentence aloud, placing the emphasis on the first word:

I didn't say he stole that money!

(Who said it?)

Continue, in the same way, but putting the emphasis on a different word each time you repeat the sentence:

I didn't ***say*** he stole that money!

(But I did think about it.)

I didn't say ***he*** stole that money!
(Maybe she did?)
I didn't say he ***stole*** that money!
(How did he get it? Did he borrow it?)
I didn't say he stole ***that*** money!
(Which money then? This money here?)
I didn't say he stole that ***money***!
(So what did he steal?)

This sentence has a number of different meanings, depending on where you place the emphasis.

Communicating effectively depends not only on being in control of *how* you say things, but of what message you are conveying when you're *not* saying anything at all. You communicate nonverbally all the time. Your body language, your gestures, even the direction that your eyes move when you are talking or listening tells people whether or not they can believe you, and how interested you are in what you're saying, how much you know.

Have you ever noticed how your eyes shift when you are trying to remember something or when you are trying to think of an answer to a question? In fact, neurophysiologically speaking, your eyes can move in nine different positions depending upon which part of your brain is activated (see Figure 12). When you look up, you are working with images; up and left means your brain is recording images; up and right, your brain is creating images.

Every time you activate the visual part of the brain, your eyes look up. If I ask you to remember the color of the blouse or shirt you wore yesterday, your eyes tend to move up in order for you to remember.

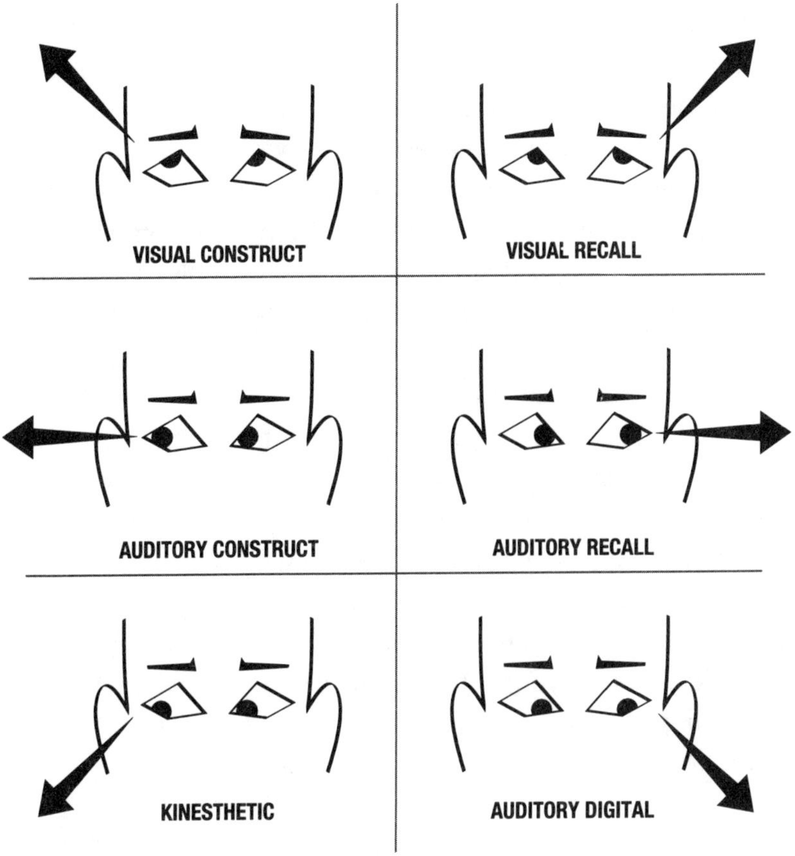

Fig. 12. Six Ways of Looking

If I talk to you and notice that your eyes are moving up, I may not know what you are thinking but I know *how* you are thinking: You've got your visual channel open. Therefore I can use a language appropriate to your visual channel, such as, "Do you see what I mean?"

When your eyes shift from side to side, your *auditory field*—sound—is coming into action; your mind is working with sounds. Looking down and to the left means you are communicating with yourself (self-talk). Looking down and to the right opens your *kinesthetic channel*, which contains feelings that you experience in your body. It's what tells you if you are tense or relaxed. When you're looking down and to the right, you also tend to have more emotions.

Depressed people tend to look down. Actually, it's quite difficult to be depressed while continuously looking upward. Think about it. And, if you want to test this mechanism, try being depressed while playing volleyball.

We utilize all our senses to communicate, some with greater or lesser strength and ability. We also respond to how others communicate with us based on our own sensory preferences. If your wife touches you to show affection when you prefer listening to her whisper in your ear, she is not going to communicate effectively with you on an emotional level. Likewise, if your husband buys you roses when what you want is a big hug, the roses will wilt before your husband ever knows he hasn't made his point.

Those of us with an auditory preference need to hear, while those of us with a visual preference need to see. Still, those of us who are more kinesthetic need to feel, to draw others close so as to sense them better. The effective communicator is aware of her impact on every level.

Like a chess game, all pieces in the communication game affect one another. Once you've moved one piece, you've changed the game.

PRINCIPLE 10

Unconditional Love

Fear is always the problem, love is always the answer

Accept other people without sitting in judgment or holding them to account for your expectations. Unconditional love means celebrating the divine intelligence that transcends all fears. This is a constant challenge, threatening the balance between reason and feelings, a balance that allows us to live in eternity today, free of past resentments and future expectations.

Loving unconditionally means seeing the future as a possibility rather than an expectation. Unfulfilled expectations generate frustration. A possibility, even when not realized, remains a possibility.

Live for today, plan for tomorrow.

CHAPTER 11

WHOM DO YOU WORK FOR?

There is only one place where success comes before work: in the dictionary.

Success demands plenty of hard work. Remember that going that extra length can win you the race. But effort and activity alone are not enough to guarantee success.

You can slave away for eighteen hours a day and never get anywhere. Like tires spinning desperately in the mud only to stay in the same spot, hard work without the right strategy will get you nowhere. A laborer toils hardest and earns least. There's no direct link between the volume of effort and the amount of money he earns. And, to make things worse, this hard worker spends so much time racing to work and getting work done that he barely has the time or energy to enjoy the rest of his life. That's surely not success.

The power to invert this relationship is in your hands. The key is to learn how to be effective. Working effectively is different from working efficiently. Efficiency means to do whatever you are doing the right way. Effectiveness means to do the right thing.

The secret of success isn't to do what you like; it's to like what you do. Work is 10 percent vocation and 90 percent adaptation. Anything can be interesting—but only you can make it so.

If you've been reading this book carefully, you will already have begun to see how it's possible to shift your perspective and change everything. What once you could only see as a problem, you can now welcome as a challenge pointed directly at you—because you can handle it. You may think you have a dull job that offers no room for creativity. You should think again. There are possibilities and opportunities right in front of you, once you learn how to see and make a commitment to them.

Here's an interesting little story from my own life. When I was a senior in medical school, I taught anatomy and physiology to the freshmen. One day the neurophysiology professor had to travel and I was asked to lecture in his place. When the professor returned, the students told him that this was the first time they understood the topic. He came to talk to me, fired with enthusiasm. He asked where I had taken the lesson from, and I showed him—his own class notes.

The professor was surprised and disappointed. The material was the same, but it was the energy and interest with which I infused the topic that made all the difference. Whatever you do wholeheartedly will have that special touch.

If you hate fitness exercises, even if someone pays you to spend the day lifting weights, you'll still loathe every minute of it. But no one has to pay bodybuilders to train—they do it because they're motivated. Perhaps when they started they had to force themselves. But as time went by, they became self-motivated, and the workout became pleasure.

To be effective at work, you have to be your own boss. Some of you might now be arguing that not everyone can run their own business or be in charge. Again, your facts might technically be right, but your perspective is wrong. The secret to working well and successfully is to work *as though* you were working for yourself. You might say, "I work for the such-and-such company." Viewing yourself as working for a person or a company is one of the worst things you can do to yourself.

You work for yourself! The company where you do your work provides you with a work area, equipment, administrative support, and other benefits, but basically it's up to you to run your own show. You know what has to get done and the best way to do it: the same way you would if the company were your own. Whether you realize it or not, you always work for yourself—no matter whether you're an employee, a department manager, or the head of the company.

From this standpoint, your value to the company is immeasurable. The more committed you are, the better the results. The better the results, the more you excel and succeed.

As you become more successful at work, more things begin to happen. The more things happen, the more work there is to do. So, what do you do now?

One of the most important secrets to effective work is to delegate. You don't always have to do things yourself to make things happen. Very few people really know how to delegate work and authority properly.

"I don't trust anyone . . ." "No one can do things as well I can." Even if you feel this way, you must delegate. And you must delegate to someone who can use the opportunity to train or learn. Never delegate to a peer or colleague; that's merely shifting the responsibility. Delegating to people who aren't up to your level gives more people the chance to learn through hands-on experience. To be effective at work, you've got to look at the bigger picture. Everyone benefits when they are surrounded by more capable people.

Being successful means knowing how to distinguish between activity and effectiveness.

Here's a story that says it all. Many years ago, people used to store old refrigerators in backyards or basements. Since these refrigerators were the ideal nook for playing hide-and-seek, children were often trapped inside. Some died of suffocation. As a result, refrigerator manufacturers began to install inner handles, and a massive educational campaign was prepared to teach children how to open the new doors.

Just as the entire system was about to be launched nationwide, someone suggested keeping refrigerator doors closed with magnets rather than locks—anyone trapped inside could escape merely by pushing against the door. All the effort and activity of the entire campaign was outweighed by the simple effectiveness of this new system.

Activity is only doing things. Effectiveness is doing what needs to be done to get the results you want.

It's good to get things done, but it's better to do the right thing. This simple change in attitude can put you in a position to earn more money and be more successful. Whenever you're poised to start any activity, pause and ask yourself, "Does this really need to be done?" And don't waste time and energy if your answer is no!

Intention without action is delusion.

PRINCIPLE 11

Harmony

Human beings are involved in an unceasing quest. We seek something to give us the feeling of peace and eternity for the moment. This grail we seek is harmony.

Harmony is the essence of existence.

Try to attune yourself to the universe, with everything and everyone around you, to the cadence of time and your own pace. Using and trusting your intuition is one way of getting in touch with the universal intelligence. By reaching harmony with yourself and the universe around you, stress vanishes from your daily life, and freedom is your reward.

CHAPTER 12

WHAT TURNS A DREAM INTO A GOAL

Many people have dreams, but dreams are different from goals. The difference is simple: Take a dream and set a target date for it to come true. Now, it's a goal. A goal is something you strive to achieve in reality. A dream remains in the realm of fantasy.

Remember that book you bought and put on the shelf to read "someday"? It's been gathering dust for years because someday doesn't appear on any calendar. When you schedule it for someday, your subconscious replies, "Sure, and when someday comes around, we'll read it!" But if you tell yourself you're going to finish it by the end of the month, you'll make time to do it.

Having clear-cut objectives in life is vital to achieving success. When you set a goal, you shape your own destiny. It's as hard to reach a goal you don't have as it is to set out on a trip without a destination.

If I have a magic wand to make your wishes come true but you can't tell me what you want because you haven't thought about it, you miss your chance. What I'm doing today is something I had in my plans ten years ago when I decided to ask myself, "What do I want?"

Do you think climbers reach the top of Mount Everest

without careful planning? Every detail must be planned in advance, with a preparation time of some four years, at a cost of several million dollars and using plenty of technology. Otherwise the expedition will die in its tracks.

Things don't happen by accident.

If you fail to have a plan, you are planning to fail.

But even some people who set goals for themselves fail to achieve them, while others manage to succeed in achieving theirs time after time. Perhaps they have some magic ability? Probably not, but maybe they use some of the techniques listed below that can increase the chances that you will become one of those who succeed in reaching your goals.

First, write your goals down.

In 1953, a survey carried out at Harvard University interviewed the graduating class. One question asked the students what they wanted to achieve in the future. This survey also asked if they had ever written down their goals. Only 3 percent answered yes. Twenty years later, they were all interviewed again. The 3 percent who had written their goals down were worth more financially than the other 97 percent together. But that's not all; they were also healthier and happier, the best-humored and best-satisfied with their lives in the entire class.

If you take out a loan, you have to sign promissory notes and a contract with the bank, complete with witnesses and guarantors. You don't just stroll up to the manager, take the money, and promise to give it back sometime.

Everything important must be written down. And isn't

your life important? But if you ask a group of people what each of them will be doing in one, two, five, or ten years, most of them will tell you they don't know and they don't have time to think about it. If you don't have time to think about the most important thing in your life—which is your life itself—then what *do* you have time to think about?

It helps to break the process down into different time periods. Set goals for the next six months, twelve months, five years, and ten years. Trust yourself, put it into practice, and see what happens.

Everything important must be written down.

Another reason you might fail to achieve your goals is that they are not really your goals. Maybe your father wanted you to study medicine but in fact you'd like to be an architect. Pursuing someone else's goal is a prescription for failure. You may succeed at first, but over the long term you won't be able to muster the willpower, energy, and stick-to-itness it takes to succeed. If you accept a goal that is not truly your own, you are guaranteeing future unhappiness.

You need to make a commitment to your goals, the same as you would to a relationship. When the going gets difficult, don't abandon hope. Try to work the problem out. Being committed means far more than just being involved. What's the difference? To get bacon and eggs for your breakfast, the hen was involved but the pig was committed.

Goals should be really big. If you tell your friends about your goals and they don't believe you, that's just about the right size. When I went to Harvard in 1976, I said to a friend that in three years I would be teaching cardiology in the

United States. He laughingly pointed out that I could barely speak English. But it took only eight months before I gave my first presentation to four hundred cardiologists in Washington, D.C. When my friend scoffed, I knew I was on the right track. If you aim for the moon, you'll still be among the stars if you miss.

A goal must be specific. What do you want? Money? But you have cash in your pocket. "Sure, but I want fifty thousand in the bank." Now your mind understands, because this is a specific request. Your mind only gets the message when you tell it exactly what you want. Then your subconscious says, "Right on, let's go for it!"

Anyone who accepts a goal that is not truly his or her own is guaranteeing future unhappiness.

Make goals for the long range. If all you think about is today, then when your boss balls you out, you'll be really upset. But if you're looking ahead—if you have a plan for five, ten, fifteen, or twenty years—you can take whatever happens today in stride.

Divide your goals into annual stages and then into even smaller pieces, so you have daily tasks that take you closer to your annual goal. You can't simply wait for your deadline and expect to find you've reached your target. That's not the way things happen. Plan seriously—because if you plan badly, you plan for failure.

Your goals should have practical benefits. Nothing vague or abstract, but a concrete target. How will your life improve when you achieve them? What will you do with the new knowledge you are pursuing?

State your goals positively. Avoid the word "don't." The way you communicate with yourself is related to how successful you are in achieving your goals. If you're not careful about the messages you give your subconscious, you may end up as what you least want to be in life.

Parents have had this experience over and over. They know that if they say, "I've told you a million times, don't tease your little sister," the child goes on disturbing the baby. With good reason—50 percent of this instruction consists of the words "tease your little sister"! The same principle applies to the phrase, "I don't want you to watch television" To "not watch television," the child's brain first has to process ". . . watch television."

If you want to change your children's attitudes, you must first adjust your language. Instead of saying, "Don't do that!" tell them, "Do this." Instead of saying, "Don't watch television," suggest they "Go play outside." This small adjustment can change your entire relationship with your children.

The same goes for the way you talk to your own subconscious. When you say that you don't want to be like your father, your subconscious bows obediently and says, "Certainly, sir: just like your father." Every time you say, "I don't want to be fat," your mind summons up visions of fat—and programs fat for your body. Instead, say, "I want to be slim," so you associate yourself with slimness instead of obesity.

Imagine how your relationship with the entire world could change if you set positive goals for your life!

Once the map is created it becomes easier to explore the territory.

PRINCIPLE 12

Knowledge and Wisdom

Intelligence serving the being

Wisdom is the intelligent use of conscious and unconscious knowledge. Its hallmarks are acute perception and flexibility in thought and action.

Developing wisdom requires wide experience combined with profound reflection. A person capable of deep inner reflection will discover the secrets of the universe, because it is there in the inner self that they lie hidden.

If what you're doing is not working, stop doing it. Reflect, analyze, and decide on a fresh course of action. To act the same way and expect different results is a sign of blindness.

CHAPTER 13

HOW TO TRANSFORM GOALS INTO REALITY

Okay, so now you understand the importance of goals in achieving success. How do you establish them? Think of the different areas of your life—work, family, financial, intellectual, to name a few. You need goals in all those spheres. The more you can enjoy and balance different kinds of experiences, the richer and more successful your life will be. To start, you have to *work* and like what you do for a living; you have to learn to *play,* because that's where creativity comes from; you have to *study* all your life, because information changes so quickly; and you have to know how to *rest.*

Here's some useful goal-setting advice—what to strive for and how not to go overboard:

- **Physical goals.** You must have a healthy body. That means eating healthfully and exercising frequently to keep yourself in good condition. But it doesn't mean that you should concentrate only on physical goals. People who devote huge amounts of time and attention to working out every day, to the detriment of other aspects of their lives, often become deeply depressed when they turn forty and note the first inevitable signs of age. As they failed to establish other objectives, their life becomes devoid of meaning.

- **Financial goals.** We live in a material world. So we must have financial goals—a certain standard of living, enough money to pay for our children's education, or enough money to travel the world.

  But, really, money itself is not the important thing; it serves only to enable us to do things that are important or pleasurable, or just plain fun. If you have no other targets in life beyond money, you may well become enslaved by the obsession to earn more and more, and end up burning out.

- **Social goals.** We all need to live within a community and to feel accepted by others. Interaction with members of a community teaches you valuable skills in how to get along with people; how to maintain and nurture friendships; and how to be less self-absorbed.

- **Professional goals.** It's vital to have interesting, stimulating work, but if you live only for your career and that long-awaited promotion never materializes, you stand a good chance of feeling like a failure.

- **Family goals.** Having warm and loving family relationships is important for mental health and general well-being. As a salve for the emotional wounds inflicted by the world, the comfort of a family cannot be overestimated. But having only family goals is not the whole answer, either. When the babies grow up—as they all do—and leave home, parents who have devoted their lives to their children to the exclusion of everything else have no way of filling their time.

- **Spiritual goals.** Whether it's a conventional religion or some form of yoga or meditation, setting spiritual goals can help you find a larger purpose in life. And by developing contact with other levels of awareness, you help yourself deal with the stresses of everyday life and unleash your creativity, to name just two benefits. If you can pinpoint your purpose in life and align your goals accordingly, the entire universe will conspire in your favor.

- **Intellectual goals.** Education is a process of continual discovery. In the information age, discovery never ends. You have to be prepared to continue discovering all your life. But again, you must keep your intellectual curiosity in balance with the rest of your life and goals. Some people try to learn the *Encyclopaedia Britannica* by heart. But they do nothing with this knowledge: They can't put it into practice, nor teach others.

These are just suggestions for the kinds of goals you might have. Make your own list—but remember not to focus too much on any one area. The happiest people are those who have a well-rounded existence.

Deciding what your goals are and being successful in reaching them is a joyous experience. To know that you can do what you set out to do fills you with a sense of accomplishment, a feeling that you control your own life. The more you experience this sense of accomplishment, the more your desire to take on new challenges increases, and the more your success grows.

Happiness comes from the same word as "to happen." Make things happen and happiness will follow.

PRINCIPLE 13

Synergy

Doing more with less

The universe is built to work by *synergy.* Synergy means the whole is greater than the sum of its parts.

Synergy means multiplying by adding. When all energies drive toward the same target, traditional arithmetic is modified: 1+1 = 4.

Synergy occurs every time two or more minds work together in a spirit of cooperation and respect, communicating and letting their intuition flow free.

CHAPTER 14

TOMORROW MORNING

Ambition is the root of all progress. Unless you really want to achieve something, you never will. Everything you do in life begins with a desire, a wish, an ambition—a conscious effort to achieve a particular goal. If someone decides there's nothing they want or need in life, they're also deciding it's time to die.

Once when a friend of mine was teaching a course on success, a gentleman in the front row rose and said, "I've been driving a cookie delivery truck for thirty years. I get up at five in the morning, make my bakery rounds, come home, wash the truck, and get everything ready for the next day. I intend to go on driving my truck until I retire. I don't want to take on new, difficult things at this stage." My friend congratulated him. He was doing exactly what he wanted to do in life.

But many people are not content with what they're doing. If you're among them, don't keep on driving your cookie truck while blaming the government, the recession, your enemies, or whatever because you haven't done more. If you go on doing what you've always done, you'll just as surely go on achieving what you've always achieved. If you want something different, do something different. Instead of blaming others for your dissatisfaction in life, you should examine yourself and find out what your deep ambition is.

When you do, it may be intimidating to realize how high your ambitions are. Faced with an obstacle or a challenge, some people recoil in horror: "No way, I couldn't do that, it's impossible!" With that attitude, even if they really try they'll never succeed, because they don't believe in themselves.

Do you know what's impossible? Something that no one can do until someone does it. Medical libraries have various tracts explaining why a man could never run a mile in under four minutes. Years of research and thousands of printed pages were all devoted to proving this limitation, until the British medical student Roger Bannister did it. In 1964, his feat made headlines around the world. Today it's commonplace, as unremarkable as saying the Earth is round.

If you go on doing what you've always done, you'll go on getting what you've always got.

When someone said it was possible to cure certain phobias in five minutes, many people said this was impossible. It was once impossible to travel from Europe to the United States in three hours but in today's supersonic jets it's normal. We live and work in a world where anything's possible. So risk a wish, and dare to try.

This doesn't mean implementing sweeping changes immediately. But minor adjustments can make a huge difference in the long run. As an airplane leaves Paris, a few degrees difference in its course can send it to either New

York or Rio de Janeiro. At takeoff, this variation is almost imperceptible; but over time it makes a tremendous difference in where you end up.

PRINCIPLE 14

The Law of Increase

Everything on which you concentrate tends to increase

Concentrate on your limitations, and they will surely grow. It's far better to concentrate on your strong points, which will grow and bear fruit.

"If you think you can, or you think you can't, you're right either way." (Henry Ford)

CHAPTER 15

PARADIGM SHIFTS: LEAPING OUT OF THE AQUARIUM

In my courses, we do not use therapies to change our behavior, but rather we work toward changing paradigms, which is far more powerful than therapy. It's the technology of the twenty-first century.

A *paradigm* is our particular way of seeing the world, a model of reality that we use to analyze events. A paradigm incorporates rules that control the way we think about a particular subject. For example, until very recently, doctors believed that stomach ulcers were a chronic irritation of the lining of the stomach caused by acids. That belief governed the way doctors treated patients and interpreted their symptoms. Because ulcers were thought to be exacerbated by stress, doctors encouraged patients to avoid situations that might bring it on. They also prescribed restrictive diets and what turned out to be ineffective medication.

Then someone discovered that ulcers are not only caused by too much stomach acid, they are also started by infections caused by bacteria. A disease that had previously been thought to be chronic was now curable, in some cases, simply through treatment with antibiotics. What had been a medical certainty was shown to be untrue, sending years of medical practice down the drain.

The new data about ulcers led to a *paradigm shift*; that is, a significant change in our understanding of something that allows us to see it in a fundamentally different way. Because it is always difficult to give up what we know, what we are used to, for something new and unfamiliar, new theories that require a paradigm shift often meet with a great deal of resistance. This was so with many of the great discoveries throughout the ages. Sometimes those revolutionaries who stretched the bounds of scientific knowledge were severely punished by established authorities.

A paradigm shift allows for new perceptions.

The philosopher and psychologist William James said that a new idea is first doomed to ridicule. It's then dismissed as trivial, until it finally becomes accepted and established as part of general knowledge. That was the case with Galileo, who determined that the sun—not the earth, as had been previously thought—was the center of our solar system. He was imprisoned and branded a heretic because, said the sages of his time, his system "runs counter to the Bible."

When Isaac Newton showed that the force of gravity that causes an apple to fall to the ground was the same force that holds the moons and the planets in their orbit, he revolutionized scientific thinking about motion. He also established, for the first time, a connection between what happens on Earth and in space. But when Einstein came around, he turned Newtonian physics on its head.

In business, it could be fatal to be trapped in an old paradigm. In 1970, the Swiss controlled 90 percent of the world's watch market. But that dominance shifted abruptly after a technician at one of Switzerland's largest watchmaking factories showed his boss a new mechanism he had invented—the electronic quartz watch. His boss examined the prototype and said, "This isn't a watch. Where's the winder? It's got no springs, no rubies." According to his paradigm, the new instrument could not be a watch.

How ironic it is that, though the inventor of the quartz mechanism was Swiss, it was the Japanese who promptly launched the electronic quartz timepiece and took over the entire market. When the paradigm changes, earlier knowledge becomes obsolete. As a result, Switzerland's 90 percent share of the market shrank to a mere 15 percent back in the early 1980s (and 50,000 Swiss watchmakers lost their jobs). Now, it's the Japanese who have to be careful not to get too comfortable in their dominance of the watchmaking market; they, too, have to be prepared not to easily dismiss any new ideas when yet another paradigm shift threatens to change their concept of "the watch."

Perception is reality; everything else is delusion.

It's not only in the giant spheres of medicine, astronomy, physics, or business that we resist new ways of seeing the world. We also have a hard time seeing ourselves differently, even when the old thinking limits our lives and causes us harm. But it is possible to see even ourselves in an entirely new way, to shift the paradigm that controls our self-perceptions, and find new strengths and abilities that we never knew we possessed. "The real act of discovery is not reaching new lands, but rather seeing them with new eyes," wrote Marcel Proust, the famous French novelist.

Those who make outstanding contributions to the progress of mankind are the ones who question the paradigms in their field and reshape them.

Paradigms are hard to change because we live within them. Does a fish know it lives in water? When we organize our lives around one particular vision, we see everything through that lens. When a scientist is faced with some fact that does not make sense within his own paradigm, he may ignore it or manipulate it until it fits into the existing rules. A surgeon tends to solve problems through surgery; a psychoanalyst through psychoanalysis. As Mark Twain said, "If your only tool is a hammer, then you treat all your problems like nails." Applying the same solution to every problem doesn't get you anywhere. Those scientists who make outstanding contributions to the progress of mankind are the ones who question the paradigms in their field and reshape them.

Here's a puzzle that illustrates how many people fail because they're trapped in the wrong paradigm. Look at Figure 13. The problem is to join all nine points together with four straight lines without lifting the pencil from the paper and without passing through the same point twice. Try a few times before you look at the solution, Figure 13A. Many people are unable to solve this puzzle because they assume that they must stay within the square. But the rules of the game don't say that. Once you alter your paradigm

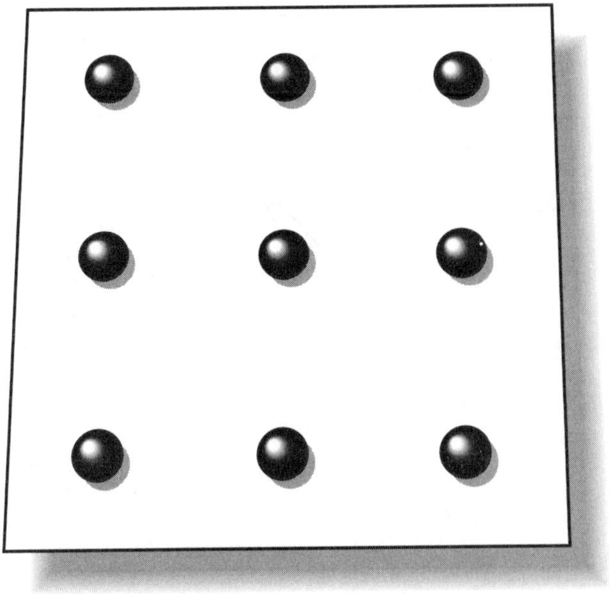

Fig. 13. Nine Dots to Join Up

and move outside what you assume are the rules, you easily find the solution.

We try to solve our problems within our own paradigms. Yet most of these paradigms are holdovers from childhood that are no longer relevant to our lives. When you lose your job because the company is restructuring to be more competitive, you might think you were laid off because you aren't good enough. That would be how you would see it if your paradigm of yourself, your frame of reference, is that you are incompetent. Obviously, you would be wrong, and that incorrect way of viewing yourself might prevent you from finding a new job. Successful people stay successful because they can shift paradigms. When one project

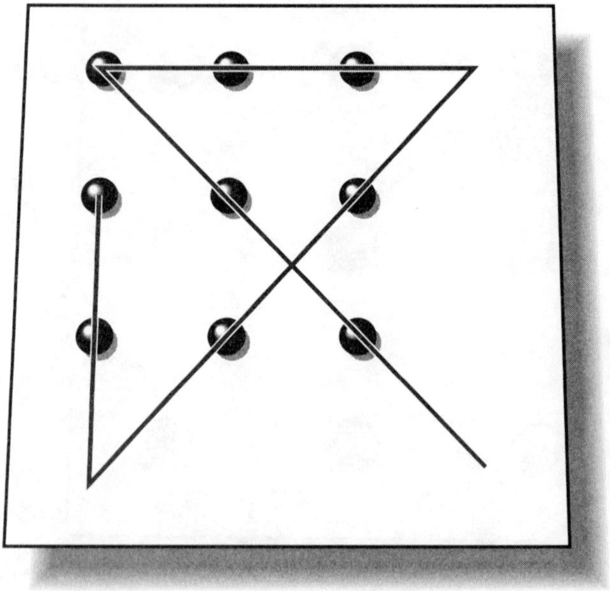

Fig. 13A. Answer

starts to fail, successful people know it's time to start moving on.

Whatever is impossible for you today may become possible if you shift the paradigm.

PRINCIPLE 15

Evolution and Development

Universal dynamics

All events in our universe take place for a reason. The basic purpose of the universe is evolution. We are all part of this evolutionary journey. Whatever happens to us is for our own good.

The only mistake we make is not to participate in this universal movement. Other than that, our so-called errors are merely feedback from the universe showing us where we are out of step.

We live in a state of constant transformation, always moving toward our final goal—harmony with everything and everyone.

Change is the only constant factor in our lives. Living is transformation, moment by moment.

CHAPTER 16

YOUR LIFE IS IN YOUR HANDS

Life is full of surprises, but that's not so surprising to the successful person, who savors life's unpredictability. Paradoxically, unpredictability is part of life's pattern. Successful people know this and have faith in the process.

The successful person knows that there are predictable and unpredictable forces that govern our lives. But they have faith that no matter what, they will succeed. Though the science of success is definable and measurable, the power unleashed when we operate according to its laws is magical.

You have so much power in you. Do I sound repetitious? If you have been following me, you already understand why I repeat myself. But do not be concerned if you're still a little confused. It takes time to assimilate new information. The truth is simple, but it must be repeated over and over again until it replaces all the destructive attitudes, illusions, and misperceptions you have been living with.

Repetition is the source of learning.

The simple truth is that if you put the understanding that I have tried to impart here into action, the returns will be enormous and unexpected. You may be skeptical; you may be thinking: How can a little thing like changing the way I talk, or devising a list of goals, make a difference? Little things *can* make a big difference.

In nature there is a complex phenomenon called *precession* that explains how certain things happen in the world. Simply put: You do one thing and something unexpected and more important results. For example, if you could ask a bee to describe its function in life, it would probably say, "To make honey." But when the bee picks up nectar from a flower to make honey, it also unintentionally pollinates the flower, which is what allows the plant to reproduce. We can all survive without honey, but not without plant life.

Successful people trust that once they take action, something good will come of it, somehow.

Almost everything good that takes place in your life happens because of this phenomenon. You don't wake up one morning and say to yourself, "Today I'm going to find a wife." You run for a bus one day and you accidentally meet your true love. To achieve anything in life, you must take action. You can never know what the end result of that action will be. But successful people trust that once they take action, something good will come of it, somehow.

Make no mistake. There is a big difference between thought and action. You have to stop saying, "When I've finished learning, I'll be ready to do things." Or, "I'm not ready yet; let me think about it a little longer." There is always more to learn, another angle to consider. Meanwhile, life slips away.

Thought and action exist in two different domains. Picturing yourself behind the steering wheel of a car is different from driving the car. Imagining the food on a menu is different from eating it.

The great writer Goethe once said, "If you think you can or dream you can, just begin. Daring has genius, power, and magic. Dare to do it and the power to do it will be granted you."

Start, get going, move it!

The life you lead is created by you and not by circumstances. Here's a little story I would like to leave you with:

In Greece there once lived a wise man who was famous for always knowing the answer to every question put to him. One day a young man said to his friend, "I think I know how to fool the sage. I'll catch a bird, hide it in my hand, and take it to the wise man. Then I'll ask him if the bird is alive or dead. If he says it's alive, I'll crush it to death and drop it on the ground. If he says it's dead,I'll open my hand and let it fly away."

The young man walked up to the sage and asked him "Wise man, is this bird in my hand alive or dead?" The sage gazed at the lad and replied, "Young man, the answer lies in your hand!"

Your life is in your hands. You can understand everything I have told you about the way the universe works and how our actions and our perceptions can be aligned with it in order to be more effective in our lives. This book offers you knowledge that can change your life. The way you use this knowledge depends on you.

Success lies in your own hands.

PRINCIPLE 16

Gratitude and Prosperity

Gratitude is the mother of all other feelings.
Give and thou shalt receive

People generally complain about what they don't have or what they've lost.

Thankfulness is in very short supply. This lack of gratitude spreads disharmony and unhappiness in our daily lives.

Offer thanks every day for what you have and the universe will give back more.

God bless you.
